Published in the United States of America by The Child's World®
PO Box 326 • Chanhassen, MN 55317-0326
800-599-READ • www.childsworld.com

My First Steps to Math™ is a registered trademark of Scholastic, Inc.

Library of Congress Cataloging-in-Publication Data
Moncure, Jane Belk.
My nine book / by Jane Belk Moncure.
p. cm. — (My first steps to math)
ISBN 1-59296-664-0 (lib. bdg. : alk. paper)
1. Counting—Juvenile literature. 2. Number concept—Juvenile literature. I. Title.
QA113.M665 2006
513.2'11—dc22
2005025699

My nine Book

by Jane Belk Moncure

illustrated by Anna DiVito

This is Little nine.

He lives in the house of nine.

The house of nine has nine rooms.

Count them.

Every day, Little  goes for a walk.

One day, he walks to the park.

He sees two toy astronauts on a bench . . .

and seven toy astronauts
sitting under a tree.

How many toy astronauts does he see?

The next day, Little  sees them again.

"We have lost our spaceships!" they say.
"We need them for the toy parade."

"I will help you," says Little nine. He hops five hops on one foot and four hops on the other foot. Can you?

Guess where he finds the first toy spaceship?

He finds the second, third, fourth, and fifth spaceships . . .

under a bridge.

Now five toy astronauts hop into their toy spaceships.

"Wait!" says Little  nine .

"Wait for the other astronauts!"
How many astronauts are missing?

Little  finds the sixth, seventh, eighth, and ninth toy spaceships in a sandbox in the park.

The four toy astronauts are happy.

Then all the toy astronauts fly away in their spaceships. Count them.

"Watch the parade!" they shout.

Little  hops six hops on one foot and three hops on the other foot. Can you?

Guess what he finds?

He finds nine toy soldiers standing in a line. They are very sad.

"The toy parade is about to begin and we have lost our nine drums," they say.

"I will help you," says Little  .

He finds six drums under a picnic table.
How many are still lost?

Now six happy soldiers beat their drums.
Tum-tum-tum, tum-tum-tum.

"Wait!" says Little nine.

"Wait for the other drummers!"
How many drummers are missing?

Little  finds . . .

two drums under the leaves . . .

and one drum

behind
a rock.

Now will each soldier have a drum?

As the happy soldiers march away, they say,

"Come to the toy parade today!"

Count the soldiers.

Then they march right down the street.
The toy parade begins at last.

Little nine waves as the soldiers march past.

The toy astronauts fly by . . .

and drop balloons from the sky.

How many balloons do they drop in all?

Little nine catches the balloons.

"I want to fly," he says.

He jumps nine high jumps. Can you?

He does not fly. *Pop, pop, pop, pop, pop* go some balloons.

How many balloons popped?

How many balloons are left?

Guess what? A real astronaut comes by.
"I will help you," she says.

"I will take you for a ride in
a real spaceship. Step inside."

"Count down! Nine, eight, seven, six, five, four, three, two, one. Blast off!"

Away they go—*ZOOM!*

Little  found nine of everything.

nine toy
astronauts

nine toy
spaceships

nine toy drums

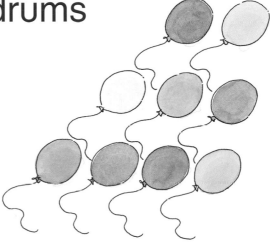

nine toy soldiers

nine balloons

Now you find nine things.

Let's add with Little  nine.

 +  =

9 + 0 = 9

 +  =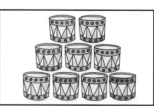

5 + 4 = 9

Now take away.

$$9 - 1 = 8$$

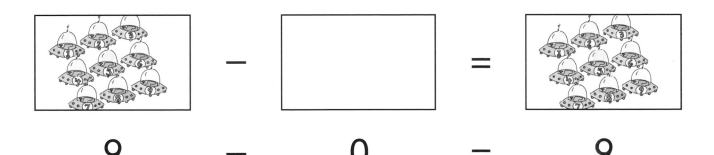

$$9 - 0 = 9$$

Little  makes a 9 this way:

He makes the number word like this:

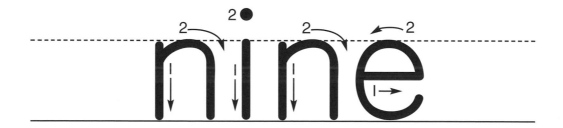

You can make them in the air with your finger.